A year in Woolly Wonders

12 quirky knitted creatures to see you through the year

Kerry Lucas

Beercott

Beercott

This book is dedicated to my nan,
without whom I may not have
discovered my love of knitting....

Contents

Introduction

Welcome to my quirky collection of woolly wonders. In this book, you will find a new creature for every month of the year, a calendar of woolly animals and birds, all native to the United Kingdom. I have always been a lover of wildlife, and as a young girl I was a keen bird watcher.

I am not sure why, but a couple of years ago I started knitting again having not used a pair of needles since I was at school, possibly spurred on by the passing of my nan who was an avid knitter. Even in her last days she was knitting blankets to send to Africa for orphaned children. Since then I haven't stopped. My first creature was a small rabbit, which has been made in various forms until I settled on the form you see in this book. Encouraged by my family and friends, I started adapting the rabbit pattern to make the other creatures, and the book is my way of sharing the fun I had along the way with other people.

Whether you create a single creature or the whole gang, I hope you have as much fun creating them as I did.

Happy knitting!

Kerry.

Materials and tools.

Most of the creatures in this book are knitted using 3mm needles and double knitting weight yarn. To complete all the patterns in this book, including the clothes and accessories for the creatures, you will need the following materials:

4mm knitting needles
3mm knitting needles
7mm knitting needles
3mm double-ended knitting needles
Stitch holders
Embroidery needle
Double knitting wool in various colours
6mm safety eyes
12mm safety eyes
Material for the dresses
Small press studs
Selection of small buttons
Toy stuffing

Abbreviations:

k: knit
p: purl
inc-kw: increase knit-wise by knitting into the front and back of the same stitch
inc-pw: increase purl-wise by purling into the front and back of the same stitch
k2tog: knit 2 together
p2tog: purl 2 together
st: stitch
stst: stocking stitch - work alternate rows of knit and purl
(n): n number of stitches
(xxx) n times: repeat (xxx) n number of times

JANUARY

Diana the Hare

Diana the Hare

Materials.

To make Diana you will need the following:

DK wool in white

DK wool in pink

2 x 6mm safety eyes

stuffing

3mm knitting needles

embroidery needle

Head

Starting at the front of the head and leaving a long end, cast on 3 st in WHITE

Row 1: inc-kw 3 times (6)
Row 2: purl
Row 3: inc-kw 6 times (12)
Row 4: purl
Row 5: (inc-kw, kw, inc-kw) 3 times (18)
Row 6: purl
Row 7: k5, inc-kw, k6, inc-kw, k5 (20)
Row 8: purl
Row 9: k6, inc-kw, k6, inc-kw, k6 (22)
Row 10: purl
Row 11: k7, inc-kw, k6, inc-kw, k7 (24)
Row 12: purl
Row 13: k8, inc-kw, k6, inc-kw, k8 (26)
Row 14: purl
Row 15: k9, inc-kw, k6, inc-kw, k9 (28)
Row 16: purl
Row 17: k9, k2tog, k6, k2tog, k9 (26)
Row 18: p8, p2tog, p6, p2tog, p8 (24)
Row 19: k7, k2tog, k6, k2tog, k7 (22)
Row 20: purl
Row 21: k2tog 11 times (11)
Row 22: p2tog twice, p3, p2tog twice (7)

Break yarn leaving a long end for sewing up the head, and place the stitches on a stitch holder.

Body

Starting at the base of the body cast on 6 st in WHITE

Row 1: inc-kw 6 times (12)
Row 2: purl
Row 3: (k1, inc-kw) 6 times (18)
Row 4: purl
Row 5: (k2, inc-kw) 6 times (24)
Row 6: purl
Row 7: k10, inc-kw, k2, inc-kw, k10 (26)
Row 8: p10, inc-pw, p1, inc-pw twice, p1, inc-pw, p10 (30)
Row 9: k10, inc-kw, k1, inc-kw, k4, inc-kw, k1, inc-kw, k10 (34)
Row 10: purl
Row 11: knit
Row 12: purl
Row 13: k10, k2tog, k1, k2tog, k4, k2tog, k1, k2tog, k10 (30)
Row 14: p10, p2tog, p1, p2tog twice, p1, p2tog, p10 (26)
Row 15: k10, k2tog, k2, k2tog, k10 (24)
Row 16-24: starting and ending with a purl row, continue in stst
Row 25: (k2, k2tog) 6 times (18)
Row 26: purl
Row 27: (k1, k2tog) 6 times (12)
Row 28: purl
Row 29: k2tog 6 times (6)

Break off yarn leaving a long end to sew up body, and transfer stitches to a stitch holder.

Arms (make 2)

Starting at the top of the arm cast on 4 st in WHITE

Row 1: inc-kw 4 times (8)
Row 2: purl
Row 3-18: continue in stst
Row 19: k2tog, inc-kw, k2, inc-kw, k2tog (8)
Row 20: purl
Row 21: k2tog, inc-kw, k2, inc-kw, k2og (8)
Row 22: purl

Break off yarn leaving a long end to sew up arm, and transfer stitches to a stitch holder.

Legs (make 2)

Starting at the top of the leg and leaving a long end, cast on 8 st in WHITE

Row 1-18: stst
Row 19: k2, inc-kw 4 times, k2 (12)
Row 20: purl
Row 21: k4, inc-kw 4 times, k4 (16)
Row 22: purl
Row 23: k6, inc-kw 4 times, k6 (20)
Row 24: purl
Row 25: k8, inc-kw 4 times, k8 (24)
Row 26: purl
Row 27: cast-off 24 kw.

Break off yarn leaving a long end

Tail

Starting at the base of the tail and leaving a long end, cast on 4 st in WHITE.

Row 1: (inc-kw) 4 times (8)
Row 2: knit
Row 3: inc-kw, k1, inc-kw, k2, inc-kw, k1, inc-kw (12)
Row 4: knit
Row 5: inc-kw, k1, inc-kw, k1, inc-kw, k2, inc-kw, k1, inc-kw, k1, inc-kw (18)
Row 6: knit
Row 7: (k2tog, k1) twice, k2tog, k2, k2tog, (k1, k2tog) twice (12)
Row 8: knit
Row 9: (k2tog) 6 times (6)
Row 10: knit
Row 11: (k2tog) 3 times (3)

Break off yarn leaving a long end and transfer stitches to a stitch holder.

Ears (make 2)

Starting at the base of the ear, cast on 5 st in WHITE

Row 1-17: (k1, p1) twice, k1
Row 18: k2tog, k1, k2tog (3)
Row 19: purl

Break off yarn leaving an end transfer stitches to a stitch holder.

To make up:

Head

Fit the safety eyes roughly half way along the head, and approximately a quarter of the width in from the edge. Thread the yarn from the last row of the head through the stitches remaining on the needle and pull tight, then remove the stitches from the needle. With right-sides together, sew along the underside of the head, leaving a small gap at the nose for stuffing. Turn the head the right way out, and stuff to the required firmness. Sew together the remaining opening and feed the end of the yarn back through the head before cutting off. Feed the remaining end back through the head before cutting off.

Body

Thread the yarn from the last row of the body through the stitches remaining on the needle and pull tight, then remove the stitches from the needle. With right-sides together, sew along the back of the body, leaving a small gap at the bottom for stuffing. Turn the body the right way out, and stuff to the required firmness. Sew together the remaining opening and feed the end of the yarn back through the body before cutting off. Feed the remaining end back through the body before cutting off.

Arms

Thread the yarn from the last row of the arm through the stitches remaining on the needle and pull tight, then remove the stitches from the needle. With right-sides together, sew along the underside of the arm, leaving a small gap at the end. Turn the arm inside out and sew up the remaining opening. Fasten off this end securely and feed back through the arm before cutting off. Weave the other loose end up through the arm and cut off the excess.

Legs

Thread the yarn from the last row of the leg through the stitches remaining on the needle and pull tight, then remove the stitches from the needle. With right-sides together, sew along the back of the leg, leaving a small gap at the foot for stuffing. Turn the leg inside out and stuff the foot lightly. Fasten off this end securely and feed back through the leg before cutting off. Weave the other loose end up through the leg and cut off the excess.

Tail

Thread the yarn from the last row of the tail through the stitches remaining on the needle and pull tight, then remove the stitches from the needle. Fold the tail in half lengthwise and sew along the edge leaving an opening at the bottom. Turn the tail inside out and stuff lightly. Sew up the opening and fasten off the yarn securely. Thread the end back through the tail before cutting off.

Assembly:

Attach the head to the body, making sure the nose points in the same direction as the stomach of the hare (the body seam should be at the back)

Attach the arms to the body just below the head, one on each side.

Attach the legs to the underside of the body, making sure the feet are facing forward.

Attach the ears to the rear of the head as in the pictures. Have the ears pointing upwards for a different expression.

Using the remaining free end, attach the tail to the rear of the body near the base.

Using a small amount of pink thread, make a few stitches at the front of the head to make a nose.

Accessories

The following accessories would fit Diana:

Waistcoat (see page 96)
Dungarees (see page 89)
Jumper (see page 90)
Hares Shoes (see page 95)

FEBRUARY

Violet the Owl

Violet the Owl

Materials.

To make Violet you will need the following:

DK wool in white

DK wool in light brown

2 x 12mm safety eyes

stuffing

3mm knitting needles

3mm double ended needles

embroidery needle

Head

Starting at base, cast on 6 st in WHITE

Row 1: inc-kw 6 times (12)
Row 2: purl
Row 3: (k1, inc-kw) 6 times (18)
Row 4: purl
Row 5: (k2, inc-kw) 6 times (24)
Row 6: purl
Row 7: (k3, inc-kw) 6 times (30)
Row 8: purl
Row 9: knit
Row 10: purl
Row 11: (k3, k2tog) 6 times (24)
Row 12: purl
Row 13: (k2, k2tog) 6 times (18)
Row 14: purl
Row 15: (k1, k2tog) 6 times (12)
Row 16: purl
Row 17: k2tog 6 times (6)

Break off yarn leaving a long end and transfer to a stitch holder.

Body

Starting at bottom Cast on 6 st in WHITE

Row 1: inc-kw 6 times (12)
Row 2: purl
Row 3: (k1, inc-kw) 6 times (18)
Row 4: purl
Row 5: (k2, inc-kw) 6 times (24)
Row 6: purl
Row 7: (k3, inc-kw) 6 times (30)
Row 8: purl
Row 9: (k4, inc-kw) 6 times (36)
Row 10: purl
Row 11: (k5, inc-kw) 6 times (42)
Row 12: purl
Row 13: knit
Row 14: purl
Row 15: knit
Row 16: purl
Row 17: (k5, k2tog) 6 times (36)
Row 18: purl
Row 19: (k4, k2tog) 6 times (30)
Row 20: purl
Row 21: (k3, k2tog) 6 times (24)
Row 22: purl
Row 23: (k2, k2tog) 6 times (18)
Row 24: purl
Row 25: (k1, k2tog) 6 times (12)
Row 26: purl
Row 27: k2tog 6 times (6)

Break off yarn leaving a long end and transfer to a stitch holder.

Wings (Make 2)

Starting at the base of the wing, cast on 3 st in WHITE

Row 1: inc-kw, k2 (4)
Row 2: knit
Row 3: inc-kw, k3 (5)
Row 4-9: knit
Row 10: inc-kw, k4 (6)
Row 11-16: knit
Row 17: inc-kw, k5 (7)
Row 18: k6, inc-kw (8)
Row 19: inc-kw, k7 (9)
Row 20: k8, inc-kw (10)
Row 21: inc-kw, k9 (11)
Row 22: knit
Row 23: k2tog, k7, k2tog (9)
Row 24: k2tog, k5, k2tog (7)
Row 25: k2tog, k3, k2tog (5)
Row 26: k2tog, k1, k2tog (3)
cast off kw. Break yarn leaving an end for sewing the wing to the body.

Beak

Starting at the base of the beak, cast on 8 st using BROWN

Row 1: knit
Row 2: k2tog, k4, k2tog (6)
Row 3: knit
Row 4: k2tog, k2, k2tog (4)
Row 5: knit
Row 6: k2tog twice (2)
Row 7: k2tog cast off kw.

Break yarn leaving an end to sew the beak together.

Repeat row 8 until the i-cord measures 65 mm overall.
Claws: continue in BROWN

Row 1: inc-kw
Put the remaining stitches on a stitch holder, then continue working i-cord on these 2 stitches as for the leg, working 4 rows in total.
Cast off kw.
Break yarn leaving an end.

Re-join yarn and work i-cord on the next 2 stiches for a total of 4 rows.
Cast off kw.
Break yarn leaving an end.

Rejoin yarn into last st and inc-kw.
Continue working i-cord on these two stitches for a total of 4 rows.
Cast-off kw leaving an end.

Legs (make 2)

Starting at the top of the leg and using 3mm double-ended needles, cast on 12 st in WHITE.

Row 1: knit
Row 2: purl
Row 3: knit
Row 4: purl
Row 5: knit
Row 6: p2tog, p8, p2tog (10)
Row 7 : k2tog, k6, k2tog (8)
Row 8: change to LIGHT BROWN, p2tog 4 times (4)
Row 9: k4

continue in i-cord as follows:

Row 8: without turning the work, move the stitches to the other end of the needle, pass the wool round the back of the work. Keeping yarn tight, k4

Tail

Starting at the point of the tail, cast on 2 st using WHITE

Row 1: inc-kw twice (4)
Rows 2-6: knit

Break off yarn and leave stitches on needle

Cast on 2 st

Row 1: inc-kw twice (4)
Rows 2-6: knit
Row 7: knit across both tail sections (8)
Rows 8-12: knit
Row 13: k2tog, k4, k2tog (6)
Row 14: Cast off kw.

Break yarn leaving an end to sew tail on to the body.

Eye feathers

Using 3mm double-ended needles cast on 3 st in WHITE and work i-cord as follows

Row 1: k3
Row 2: without turning the work, move the stitches to the other end of the needle, pass the wool round the back of the work. Keeping yarn tight, k3

Continue in this way until the cord measures 55mm then cast-off kw.

To make up

Head

Fit the safety eyes roughly in the middle of the head, and close together. Thread the yarn from the last row of the head through the stitches remaining on the needle and pull tight, then remove the stitches from the needle. With right-sides together, sew along the back of the head, leaving a small gap at the base for stuffing. Turn the head the right way out, and stuff to the required firmness. Sew together the remaining opening and feed the end of the yarn back through the head before cutting off. Feed the remaining end back through the head before cutting off.

Body

Thread the yarn from the last row of the body through the stitches remaining on the needle and pull tight, then remove the stitches from the needle. With right-sides together, sew along the back of the body, leaving a small gap at the bottom for stuffing. Turn the body the right way out, and stuff to the required firmness. Sew together the remaining opening and feed the end of the yarn back through the body before cutting off. Feed the remaining end back through the body before cutting off.

Legs

Thread the yarn from the last row of each claw back through the claw and cut. fasten off the threads at the base of each claw, and then feed the ends up the leg before trimming. Sew down the back of the upper leg, and stuff lightly before sewing across the top of the leg and fastening off.

Beak

Fold the beak in half, and sew together along the edge to form a triangle, leaving the cast-on edge open. Feed the thread back through the beak before trimming.

Assembly:

Attach the head to the body, making sure the eyes point forward (the body seam should be at the back).

Sew the beak to the front of the head between and just below the eyes, adding a little stuffing if desired.

Using the free thread, sew the wings to the sides of the body in the position shown.

Using the free thread, attach the legs to the underside of the body, making sure the seam on the upper leg is facing towards the back.

Using the free thread, attach the tail to the back of the body, towards the bottom as shown.

Attach the eye feathers to the head around the eyes as shown in the pictures.

Accessories

The following accessories would be suitable for Violet:

Scarf (see page 97)
Shawl (see page 97)

MARCH

Blue and Belle the Rabbits

Blue & Belle the Rabbits

Materials.

To make Blue or Belle you will need the following:

DK wool in grey

DK wool in pink

2 x 6mm safety eyes

stuffing

3mm knitting needles

3mm double ended needles

embroidery needle

Head

Starting at the nose, cast on 3 st in GREY

Row 1: (inc-kw) 3 times (6)
Row 2: purl
Row 3: (inc-kw) 6 times (12)
Row 4: purl
Row 5: (inc-kw, k2, inc-kw) 3 times (18)
Row 6: purl
Row 7: k5, inc-kw, k6, inc-kw, k5 (20)
Row 8: purl
Row 9: k6, inc-kw, k6, inc-kw, k6 (22)
Row 10-20: starting and ending with a purl row, continue in stst
Row 21: (k2tog) 11 times (11)
Row 22: (p2tog) twice, p3, (p2tog) twice (7)

Break off yarn leaving a long end and transfer stitches to a stitch holder.

Body

Starting at the base of the body, cast on 6 st in GREY

Row 1: (inc-kw) 6 times (12)
Row 2: purl
Row 3: (k1, inc-kw) 6 times (18)
Row 4: purl
Row 5: (k2, inc-kw) 6 times (24)
Row 6-26: continue in stst starting and ending with a purl row
Row 27: (k2, k2tog) 6 times (18)
Row 28: purl
Row 29: (k1, k2tog) 6 times (12)
Row 30: purl
Row 31: (k2tog) 6 times (6)

Break off yarn leaving a long end and transfer stitches to a stitch holder.

Arms (make 2)

Using 3mm double-ended needles and leaving a long end, cast on 3 st using GREY and work i-cord as follows

Row 1: k3
Row 2: without turning the work, move the stitches to the other end of the needle, pass the wool round the back of the work. Keeping yarn tight, k3
Repeat row 2 until the arm measures 85mm.

Break off yarn leaving a long end, and transfer stitches to a stitch holder.

Legs (make 2)

Using 3mm double-ended needles and leaving a long end, cast on 4 st using GREY and work i-cord as follows

Row 1: k4
Row 2: without turning the work, move the stitches to the other end of the needle, pass the wool round the back of the work. Keeping yarn tight, k4
Repeat row 2 until the leg measures 95mm.

Break off yarn leaving a long end, and transfer stitches to a stitch holder

Ears (make 2)

Using 3mm needles cast on 5st in GREY

Row 1-17: (k1, p1) twice, k1
Row 18: k2tog, k1, k2tog (3)
Row 19: purl

Break off yarn leaving an end and transfer stitches to a stitch holder.

Tail

Starting at the base of the tail and leaving a long end, cast on 4st in GREY.

Row 1: (inc-kw) 4 times (8)

Row 2: knit
Row 3: inc-kw, k1, inc-kw, k2, inc-kw, k1, inc-kw (12)
Row 4: knit
Row 5: inc-kw, k1, inc-kw, k1, inc-kw, k2, inc-kw, k1, inc-kw, k1, inc-kw (18)
Row 6: knit
Row 7: k2tog, k1, k2tog, k1, k2tog, k2, k2tog, k1, k2tog, k1, k2tog (12)
Row 8: knit
Row 9: k2tog, k1, k2tog, k2, k2tog, k1, k2tog (8)
Row 10: knit
Row 11: (k2tog) 4 times (4)
Cast-off kw.

Break off yarn leaving a long end and transfer stitches to a stitch holder.

To make up

Head

Fit the safety eyes roughly a third of the way along the head from the nose, and roughly a quarter of the way in from each side. Thread the yarn from the last row of the head through the stitches remaining on the needle and pull tight, then remove the stitches from the needle. With right-sides together, sew along the base of the head, leaving a small gap at the nose for stuffing.
Turn the head the right way out, and stuff to the required firmness. Sew together the remaining opening and feed the end of the yarn back through the head before cutting off. Feed the remaining end back through the head before cutting off.

Body

Thread the yarn from the last row of the body through the stitches remaining on the needle and pull tight,

then remove the stitches from the needle. With right-sides together, sew along the back of the body, leaving a small gap at the bottom for stuffing. Turn the body the right way out, and stuff to the required firmness. Sew together the remaining opening and feed the end of the yarn back through the body before cutting off. Feed the remaining end back through the body before cutting off.

Arms

Thread the yarn from the last row of the arm through the stitches remaining on the needle and pull tight, then remove the stitches from the needle. Fasten off this end securely. Weave the other loose end up through the arm and cut off the excess.

Legs

Thread the yarn from the last row of the leg through the stitches remaining on the needle and pull tight, then remove the stitches from the needle. Fasten off this end securely. Weave the other loose end up through the leg and cut off the excess.

Ears

Thread the yarn from the last row of the ear through the stitches remaining on the needle and pull tight, then remove the stitches from the needle. Fasten off this end securely. Thread the other end through the ear before cutting off.

Tail

Thread the free end of the tail round the edge of the tail in a running stitch. Pull the thread to gather the tail, stuffing lightly to form a ball. Fasten off this end securely. Thread the end back through the tail before cutting off.

Assembly:

Attach the head to the body, making sure the nose points forward (the body seam should be at the back)

Using the free thread, attach the arms to the body just below the head, one on each side.

Using the free thread, attach the legs to the underside of the body.

Using the free end, attach the ears to the rear of the head, one on either side as in the pictures.

Using the free thread, attach the tail to the rear of the body near the bottom.

Using a small amount of pink thread, make a few stitches at the front of the head to make a nose.

Accessories

The following accessories would be suitable for the rabbits:

Dress (see page 92)
Cardigan (see page 88)
Dungarees (see page 89)
Boots (see page 95)

Scarf (see page 97)
Shawl (see page (97)

APRIL

Daisy the Deer

Daisy the Deer

Materials.

To make Daisy you will need the following:

DK wool in black

DK wool in light brown

2 x 6mm safety eyes

stuffing

3mm knitting needles

3mm double ended needles

embroidery needle

Head

Starting at the nose and leaving a long end, cast on 3 st using BLACK

Row 1: inc-kw 3 times (6)
Row 2: purl
Row 3: inc-kw 6 times (12)
Row 4: purl
Row 5: change to LIGHT BROWN, (inc-kw, k2, inc-kw) 3 times (18)
Row 6: purl
Row 7: k5, inc-kw, k6, inc-kw, k5 (20)
Row 8: purl
Row 9: k6, inc-kw, k6, inc-kw, k6 (22)
Row 10: purl
Row 11: k7, inc-kw, k6, inc-kw, k7 (24)
Row 12: purl
Row 13: k8, inc-kw, k6, inc-kw, k8 (26)
Row 14: purl
Row 15: k9, inc-kw, k6, inc-kw, k9 (28)
Row 16: purl
Row 17: k9, k2tog, k6, k2tog, k9 (26)
Row 18: p8, p2tog, p6, p2tog, p8 (24)
Row 19: k7, k2tog, k6, k2tog, k7 (22)

Row 20: purl
Row 21: (k2tog) 11 times (11)
Row 22: (p2tog twice), p3, (p2tog) twice (7)

Break yarn leaving a long end for sewing up the head, and place the stitches on a stitch holder.

Body

Starting at the base of the body cast on 6 st in LIGHT BROWN

Row 1: inc-kw 6 times (12)
Row 2: purl
Row 3: (k1, inc-kw) 6 times (18)
Row 4: purl
Row 5: (k2, inc-kw) 6 times (24)
Row 6: purl
Row 7: k10, inc-kw, k2, inc-kw, k10 (26)
Row 8: p10, inc-pw, p1, inc-pw twice, p1, inc-pw, p10 (30)
Row 9: k10, inc-kw, k1, inc-kw, k4, inc-kw, k1, inc-kw, k10 (34)
Row 10: purl
Row 11: knit
Row 12: purl
Row 13: k10, k2tog, k1, k2tog, k4, k2tog, k1, k2tog, k10 (30)
Row 14: p10, p2tog, p1, p2tog twice, p1, p2tog, p10 (26)
Row 15: k10, k2tog, k2, k2tog, k10 (24)
Row 16-24: starting and ending with a purl row, continue in stst.
Row 25: (k2, k2tog) 6 times (18)
Row 26: purl
Row 27: (k1, k2tog) 6 times (12)
Row 28: purl

Row 29: k2tog 6 times (6)

Break off yarn leaving a long end to sew up body, and transfer stitches to a stitch holder.

Arms (make 2)

Using 3mm double-ended needles and leaving a long end, cast on 3 st using LIGHT BROWN and work i-cord as follows

Row 1: k3
Row 2: without turning the work, move the stitches to the other end of the needle, pass the wool round the back of the work. Keeping yarn tight, k3

Repeat row 2 until the arm measures 85mm.

Break off yarn leaving a long end, and transfer stitches to a stitch holder

Legs (make 2)

Using 3mm double-ended needles and leaving a long end, cast on 4 st using LIGHT BROWN and work i-cord as follows

Row 1: k4
Row 2: without turning the work, move the stitches to the other end of the needle, pass the wool round the back of the work. Keeping yarn tight, k4
Repeat row 2 until the arm measures 95mm.

Break off yarn leaving a long end, and transfer stitches to a stitch holder.

Antlers (make 2)

Using 3mm double-ended needles and leaving a long end, cast on 4 st using LIGHT BROWN and work i-cord as follows

Row 1: k4
Row 2: without turning the work, move the stitches to the other end of the needle, pass the wool round the back of the work. Keeping yarn tight, k4

Repeat row 2 until the antler measures 24mm.

Branch

Row 1: k2, then put the remaining 2 st on a stitch holder.

Continue in i-cord on these 2 stiches for 3 rows.
Cast off kw. Break off yarn.

Re-join yarn and work i-cord on the last 2 stitches for 6 rows.
Cast-off kw. Break off yarn.

Tail

Starting at the base of the tail and leaving a long end, cast on 4 st in LIGHT BROWN.

Row 1: (inc-kw) 4 times (8)
Row 2: knit
Row 3: inc-kw, k1, inc-kw, k2, inc-kw, k1, inc-kw (12)
Row 4: knit
Row 5: inc-kw, k1, inc-kw, k1, inc-kw, k2, inc-kw, k1, inc-kw, k1, inc-kw (18)
Row 6: knit
Row 7: (k2tog, k1) twice, k2tog, k2, k2tog, (k1, k2tog) twice (12)
Row 8: knit
Row 9: (k2tog) 6 times (6)
Row 10: knit
Row 11: (k2tog) 3 times (3)

Break off yarn leaving a long end and transfer stitches to a stitch holder.

Ears (make 2)

Cast on 6 st using LIGHT BROWN

Row 1-3: knit
Row 4: k2tog, k2, k2tog (4)
Row 5: (k2tog) twice (2)
Row 6: k2tog (1)
Row 7:Cast off kw.

To make up

Head

Fit the safety eyes roughly a third of the way along the head from the nose, and roughly a quarter of the way in from each side. Thread the yarn from the last row of the head through the stitches remaining on the needle and pull tight, then remove the stitches from the needle. With right-sides together, sew along the base of the head, leaving a small gap at the nose for stuffing.
Turn the head the right way out, and stuff to the required firmness. Sew together the remaining opening and feed the end of the yarn back through the head before cutting off. Feed the remaining end back through the head before cutting off.

Body

Thread the yarn from the last row of the body through the stitches remaining on the needle and pull tight, then remove the stitches from the needle. With right-sides together, sew along the back of the body, leaving a small gap at the bottom for stuffing. Turn the body the right way out, and stuff to the required firmness. Sew together the remaining opening and feed the end of the yarn back through the body before cutting off. Feed the remaining end back through the body before cutting off.

Arms

Thread the yarn from the last row of the arm through the stitches remaining on the needle and pull tight, then remove the stitches from the needle. Fasten off this end securely. Weave the other loose end up through the arm and cut off the excess.

Legs

Thread the yarn from the last row of the leg through the stitches remaining on the needle and pull tight, then remove the stitches from the needle. Fasten off this end securely. Weave the other loose end up through the leg and cut off the excess.

Ears

Thread the yarn from the last row of the ear through the side of the ear before cutting off. Fold the ear in half length-wise and join across the bottom.

Tail

Thread the yarn from the last row of the tail through the stitches remaining on the needle and pull tight, then remove the stitches from the needle. Fold the tail in half lengthwise and sew along the edge leaving an opening at the bottom. Turn the tail inside out and stuff lightly. Sew up the opening and fasten off the yarn securely. Thread the end back through the tail before cutting off.

Antlers

Thread the yarn from the last row of each branch back through the antler and cut. Fasten off the threads at the base of each branch, and then feed the ends up the antler before trimming.

Assembly:

Attach the head to the body, making sure the nose points in the same direction as the stomach of the deer (the body seam should be at the back)
Using the free thread, attach the arms to the body just below the head, one on each side.

Using the free thread, attach the legs to the underside of the body.

Using the free end, attach the ears to the rear of the head, one on either side as in the pictures.

Using the free end, sew each antler to the top of the head between the ears, making sure the short branches face in opposite directions or forward.

Using the free thread, attach the tail to the rear of the body near the bottom, with the point facing upwards.

Accessories

The following accessories would be suitable for Daisy:

Dress (see page 92)
Cardigan (see page 88)
Dungarees (see page 89)
Boots (see page 95)
Scarf (see page 97)
Shawl (see page 97)

MAY

Patrick the Frog

Patrick the frog.

Materials.

To make Patrick you will need the following:

DK wool in green

DK wool in black for the mouth

2 x 12mm black safety eyes

stuffing

3mm knitting needles

3mm double ended needles

embroidery needle

Head.

Starting at the front of the head and leaving a long end, cast on 3 st

Row 1: inc-kw 3 times (6)

Row 2: purl

Row 3: inc-kw 6 times (12)

Row 4: purl

Row 5: (inc-kw, k2, inc-kw) 3 times (18)

Row 6: purl

Row 7: k5, inc-kw, k6, inc-kw, k5 (20)

Row 8: purl

Row 9: k6, inc-kw, k6, inc-kw, k6 (22)

Row 10: purl

Row 11: k7, inc-kw, k6, inc-kw, k7 (24)

Row 12: purl

Row 13: k8, inc-kw, k6, inc-kw, k8 (26)

Row 14: purl

Row 15: k9, inc-kw, k6, inc-kw, k9 (28)

Row 16: purl

Row 17: k2tog, k3, k2tog, k2, k2tog, k6, k2tog, k2, k2tog, k3, k2tog (22)

Row 18: p2tog 11 times (11)

Row 19: k2tog, k1, k2tog, k1, k2tog, k1, k2tog (7)

Break yarn leaving a long end for sewing up the head, and place the stitches on a stitch holder.

Body.

Starting at the base of the body cast on 6 st

Row 1: inc-kw 6 times (12)
Row 2: purl
Row 3: (k1, inc-kw) 6 times (18)
Row 4: purl
Row 5: (k2, inc-kw) 6 times (24)
Row 6: purl
Row 7: k10, inc-kw, k2, inc-kw, k10 (26)
Row 8: p10, inc-pw, p1, inc-pw twice, p1, inc-pw, p10 (30)
Row 9: k10, inc-kw, k1, inc-kw, k4, inc-kw, k1, inc-kw, k10 (34)
Row 10: purl
Row 11: knit
Row 12: purl
Row 13: k10, k2tog, k1, k2tog, k4, k2tog, k1, k2tog, k10 (30)
Row 14: p10, p2tog, p1, p2tog twice, p1, p2tog, p10 (26)
Row 15: k10, k2tog, k2, k2tog, k10 (24)
Row 16: purl
Row 17: knit
Row 18: purl
Row 19: knit
Row 20: purl
Row 21: knit
Row 22: purl
Row 23: knit
Row 24: purl
Row 25: (k2, k2tog) 6 times (18)
Row 26: purl
Row 27: (k1, k2tog) 6 times (12)
Row 28: purl
Row 29: k2tog 6 times (6)

Break off yarn leaving a long end to sew up body, and transfer stitches to a stitch holder.

Arms (make 2)

Using 3mm double-ended needles and leaving a long end, cast on 3 st and work i-cord as follows

Row 1: k3
Row 2: without turning the work, move the stitches to the other end of the needle, pass the wool round the back of the work. Keeping yarn tight, k3

Continue like this until the arm measures 85mm.
Break off yarn leaving a long end, and transfer stitches to a stitch holder.

Legs (make 2)

Using 3mm double-ended needles and leaving a long end, cast on 4 st and work i-cord as follows

Row 1: k4
Row 2: without turning the work, move the stitches to the other end of the needle, pass the wool round the back of the work. Keeping yarn tight, k4

Continue like this until the leg measures 105mm.

Foot:

Work normally, turning the work after each row

Row 1: k3, inc-kw (5)
Row 2: k1, p1, k1, p1, k1
Row 3: p1, inc-kw, p1, inc-kw, p1 (7)
Row 4: k1, p2, k1, p2, k1
Row 5: p1, k1, inc-kw, p1, inc-kw, k1, p1 (9)
Row 6: k1, p3, k1, p3, k1
Row 7: p1, k1, inc-kw, k1, p1, k1, inc-kw, k1, p1 (11)
Row 8: k1, p4, k1, p4, k1
Row 9: p1, inc-kw, k1, inc-kw, k1, p1, k1, inc-kw, k1, inc-kw, p1 (15)
Row 10: k1, p6, k1, p6, k1
Row 11: cast-off 1 pw, cast-off 6 kw, cast-off 1 pw, cast-off 6-kw, cast-off 1 pw

Break off yarn leaving a long end. Tie a knot in the middle of the leg to form the knee.

Eyebrows (make 2)

Using 3mm double-ended needles and leaving a long end, cast on 3 st and work i-cord as follows

Row 1: k3
Row 2: without turning the work, move the stitches to the other end of the needle, pass the wool round the back of the work. Keeping yarn tight, k3

Continue in this way until the eyebrow measures 30mm

Break off yarn leaving a long end and transfer stitches to a stitch holder

To make up:

Head

Fit the safety eyes roughly half way along the head, and approximately a quarter of the width in from the edge. Thread the yarn from the last row of the head through the stitches remaining on the needle and pull tight, then remove the stitches from the needle. With right-sides together, sew along the underside of the head, leaving a small gap at the nose for stuffing. Turn the head the right way out, and stuff to the required firmness. Sew together the remaining opening and feed the end of the yarn back through the head before cutting off. Feed the remaining end back through the head before cutting off.

Body

Thread the yarn from the last row of the body through the stitches remaining on the needle and pull tight, then remove the stitches from the needle. With right-sides together, sew along the back of the body, leaving a small gap at the bottom for stuffing. Turn the body the right way out, and stuff to the required firmness. Sew together the remaining opening and feed the end of the yarn back through the body before cutting off. Feed the remaining end back through the body before cutting off.

Arms

Thread the yarn from the last row of the arm through the stitches remaining on the needle and pull tight, then remove the stitches from the needle. Fasten off this end securely. Weave the other loose end up through the arm and cut off the excess.

Legs

Thread the yarn from the last row of the leg through the stitches remaining on the needle and pull tight, then remove the stitches from the needle. Fasten off this end securely. Weave the other loose end up through the leg and cut off the excess. Tie a knot halfway up the leg to make the knee.

Eyebrows

Thread the yarn from the last row of the head through the stitches remaining on the needle and pull tight, then remove the stitches from the needle. Fasten off this end securely. Weave the other loose end up through the eyebrow and cut off the excess.

Assembly:

Attach the head to the body, making sure the nose points in the same direction as the stomach of the frog (the body seam should be at the back)

Using the free thread, attach the arms to the body just below the head, one on each side.

Using the free thread, attach the legs to the underside of the body, making sure the ridges on the feet that form the toes are facing forward.

Using the free thread, attach the eyebrows to the head so that they curl round the eyes as shown in the picture.

Using black yarn, sew a couple of stitches on the front of the head to make the mouth.

Accessories

Any of the accessories in the book will fit Patrick, but I would suggest the following options:

Waistcoat (see page 96)
Dungarees (see page 89)

JUNE

Rose the Fox

Rose the Fox

Materials.

To make Rose you will need the following:

DK wool in red

DK wool in black

DK wool in white

2 x 6mm black safety eyes

stuffing

3mm knitting needles

embroidery needle

For loop stitch, see page 98

Head

Starting at the nose and leaving a long end, cast on 3 st using BLACK

Row 1: inc-kw 3 times (6)
Row 2: purl
Row 3: inc-kw 6 times (12)
Row 4: purl
Row 5: change to RED, (inc-kw, k2, inc-kw) 3 times (18)
Row 6: purl
Row 7: k5, inc-kw, k6, inc-kw, k5 (20)
Row 8: purl
Row 9: k6, inc-kw, k6, inc-kw, k6 (22)
Row 10: purl
Row 11: k7, inc-kw, k6, inc-kw, k7 (24)
Row 12: purl
Row 13: k8, inc-kw, k6, inc-kw, k8 (26)
Row 14: purl
Row 15: k9, inc-kw, k6, inc-kw, k9 (28)
Row 16: purl
Row 17: k9, k2tog, k6, k2tog, k9 (26)
Row 18: p8, p2tog, p6, p2tog, p8 (24)

Row 19: k7, k2tog, k6, k2tog, k7 (22)
Row 20: purl
Row 21: (k2tog) 11 times (11)
Row 22: (p2tog twice), p3, (p2tog) twice (7)

Break yarn leaving a long end for sewing up the head, and place the stitches on a stitch holder.

Belly

Starting at the bottom of the belly and leaving a long end, cast on 3 st using RED

Row 1: inc-kw 3 times (6)
Row 2: change to WHITE and purl
Row 3: k2, (inc-kw) twice, k2 (8)
Row 4: purl
Row 5: k2, inc-kw, k2, inc-kw, k2 (10)
Row 6: purl
Row 7: k2, inc-kw, k4, inc-kw, k2 (12)
Row 8: p2, inc-pw, p6, inc-pw, p2 (14)
Row 9: knit
Row 10: purl
Row 11: knit
Row 12: purl
Row 13: k2, k2tog, k6, k2tog, k2 (12)
Row 14: p2, p2tog, p4, p2tog, p2 (10)
Row 15: k2, k2tog, k2, k2tog, k2 (8)
Row 16: purl
Row 17: knit
Row 18: purl
Row 19: knit
Row 20: purl
Row 21: knit
Row 22: purl
Row 23: knit
Row 24: purl
Row 25: k1, (k2tog, k1) twice, k1 (6)
Row 26: purl
Row 27: change to RED, (k1, k2tog) twice (4)
Row 28: purl

Row 29: k2tog twice (2)
Row 30: cast-off kw.

Break off yarn leaving a long end.

Back

Starting at the bottom of the back and leaving a long end, cast on 5 st using RED

Row 1: inc-kw 5 times (10)
Row 2: purl
Row 3: (k1, inc-kw) 5 times (15)
Row 4: purl
Row 5: (k2, inc-kw, k2, inc-w) twice, k2, inc-kw (20)
Row 6: purl
Row 7-24:starting with a knit row, continue in stst
Row 25: (k2, k2tog) 4 times, k2tog, k2 (15)
Row 26: purl
Row 27: (k1, k2tog) 5 times (10)
Row 28: (p1, p2tog) 3 times, p1 (7)
Row 29: (k1, k2tog) twice, k1 (5)
Row 30: cast-off pw.

Break off yarn leaving a long end.

Arms (make 2)

Using 3mm double-ended needles and leaving a long end, cast on 3 st using RED and work i-cord as follows

Row 1: k3
Row 2: without turning the work, move the stitches to the other end of the needle, pass the wool round the back of the work. Keeping yarn tight, k3

Repeat row 2 until the arm measures 85mm.
Break off yarn leaving a long end, and transfer stitches to a stitch holder

Legs (make 2)

Using 3mm double-ended needles and leaving a long end, cast on 4 st in RED and work i-cord as follows

Row 1: k4
Row 2: without turning the work, move the stitches to the other end of the needle, pass the wool round the back of the work. Keeping yarn tight, k4

Repeat row 2 until the leg measures 95mm.
Break off yarn leaving a long end, and transfer stitches to a stitch holder

Ears (make 2)

Cast on 6 st using RED

Row 1-3: knit
Row 4: k2tog, k2, k2tog (4)
Row 5: (k2tog) twice (2)
Row 6: k2tog (1)
Row 7:Cast off kw.

Tail

Starting at the base of the tail cast on 4 st in RED

Row 1: inc-kw 4 times (8)
Row 2: purl
Row 3: k1, loop st 6 times, k1
Row 4: purl
Row 5: k1, loop st 6 times, k1
Row 6: purl
Row 7: k1, loop st 6 times, k1
Row 8: purl
Row 9: k1, loop st 6 times, k1
Row 10: purl
Row 11: k1, loop st 6 times, k1
Row 12: purl

Row 13: k1, loop st 6 times, k1
Row 14: purl
Row 15: k1, loop st 6 times, k1
Row 16: purl
Row 17: k1, loop st 6 times, k1
Row 18: purl
Row 19: change to WHITE, k1, loop st 6 times, k1
Row 20: purl
Row 21: k1, loop st 6 times, k1
Row 22: purl
Row 23: k2tog 4 times (4)

Break yarn leaving a long end and transfer stitches to a stitch holder

To make up

Head

Fit the safety eyes roughly half way along the head, and approximately a quarter of the width in from the edge. Thread the yarn from the last row of the head through the stitches remaining on the needle and pull tight, then remove the stitches from the needle. With right-sides together, sew along the underside of the head, leaving a small gap at the nose for stuffing. Turn the head the right way out, and stuff to the required firmness. Sew together the remaining opening and feed the end of the yarn back through the head before cutting off. Feed the remaining end back through the head before cutting off.

Body

With right sides together, sew the belly to the back down each side. Run a thread round the neck using a running stitch and gather, then fasten off.
Turn the body right-side out and stuff.

Sew up the bottom opening.
Thread the remaining end back up through the body before cutting off.

Arms

Thread the yarn from the last row of the arm through the stitches remaining on the needle and pull tight, then remove the stitches from the needle. Fasten off this end securely. Weave the other loose end up through the arm and cut off the excess.

Legs

Thread the yarn from the last row of the leg through the stitches remaining on the needle and pull tight, then remove the stitches from the needle. Fasten off this end securely. Weave the other loose end up through the leg and cut off the excess.

Ears

Fasten off the end at the top of the ear, and weave through the ear before cutting off.

Tail

Fold the tail in half with the loops on the outside. Sew up the edge of the tail. Fasten off and pass the free end of the yarn up through the tail before trimming off.

Assembly:

Attach the head to the body, making sure the nose points in the same direction as the stomach of the fox

Using the free thread, attach the arms to the body just below the head, one on each side.

Using the free thread, attach the legs to the underside of the body.

Using the free end, attach the ears to the rear of the head, one on either side as in the pictures.

Using the free thread, attach the tail to the rear of the body near the bottom.

Accessories

I would suggest the following accessories for Rose:

Dress (see page 92)
Cardigan (see page 88)
Boots (see page 95)

JULY

Brian the Blackbird

Brian the blackbird.

Materials.

To make Brian you will need the following:

DK wool in black

DK wool in light brown

DK wool in yellow

2 x 6mm safety eyes

stuffing

3mm knitting needles

3mm double ended needles

embroidery needle

Head.

Starting at the front of the head and leaving a long end, cast on 3 st using BLACK and 3mm needles

Row 1: inc-kw 3 times (6)
Row 2: purl
Row 3: inc-kw 6 times (12)
Row 4: purl
Row 5: (inc-kw, k2, inc-kw) 3 times (18)
Row 6: purl
Row 7: k5, inc-kw, k6 inc-kw, k5 (20)
Row 8: Purl
Row 9: K6, inc-kw, k6, inc-kw, k6 (22)
Row 10-16: starting and ending with a purl row, continue in stst
Row 17: k2tog 11 times (11)
Row 18: p2tog twice, p3, p2tog twice (7)

Break yarn leaving a long end for sewing up the head, and place the stitches on a stitch holder.

Body

Starting at the base of the body cast on 6 st using BLACK and 3mm needles

Row 1: inc-kw 6 times (12)
Row 2: purl
Row 3: (k1, inc-kw) 6 times (18)
Row 4: purl
Row 5: (K2, inc-kw) 6 times (24)
Row 6-24: starting and ending with a purl row, continue in stst
Row 25: (k2, k2tog) 6 times (18)
Row 26: purl
Row 27: (k1, k2tog) 6 times (12)
Row 28: purl
Row 29: k2tog 6 times (6)

Break off yarn leaving a long end to sew up body, and transfer stitches to a stitch holder.

Legs (make 2)

Using 3mm double-ended needles and leaving a long end, cast on 4 st in LIGHT BROWN and work i-cord as follows

Row 1: k4
Row 2: without turning the work, move the stitches to the other end of the needle, pass the wool round the back of the work. Keeping yarn tight, k4

Continue like this until the leg measures 105mm.

Claws: continue in LIGHT BROWN

Row 1: inc-kw

Put the remaining stitches on a stitch holder, then continue working i-cord on these 2 stitches as for the leg, working 4 rows in total.
Cast off kw.
Break yarn leaving an end.

Re-join yarn and work i-cord on the next 2 stiches for a total of 4 rows.
Cast off kw.
Break yarn leaving an end.

Rejoin yarn into last st and inc-kw.
Continue working i-cord on these two stitches.
Cast-off kw leaving an end.

Tail

Using BLACK and 3mm needles cast on 2 st
Row 1: inc-kw twice (4)
Rows 2-8: knit
Break off yarn and leave stitches on needle

Cast on 2 st
Row 1: inc-kw twice (4)
Rows 2-8: knit
Row 9: knit across both tail sections (8)
Rows 10-14: knit
Row 15: k2tog, 4, k2tog (6)
cast off kw. Break yarn leaving an end to sew tail on to the body.

Wings (Make 2)

Using BLACK and 3mm needles cast on 3 st.

Row 1: inc-kw, k2 (4)
Row 2: knit
Row 3: inc-kw, k3 (5)
Row 4-9: knit
Row 10: inc-kw, k4 (6)
Row 11-16: knit
Row 17: inc-kw, k5 (7)
Row 18: k6, inc-kw (8)
Row 19: inc-kw, k7 (9)
Row 20: k8, inc-kw (10)
Row 21: inc-kw, k9 (11)
Row 22: knit
Row 23: k2tog, k7, k2tog (9)
Row 24: k2tog, k5, k2tog (7)
Row 25: k2tog, k3, k2tog (5)
Row 26: k2tog, k1, k2tog (3)

cast off kw. Break yarn leaving an end for sewing the wing to the body.

Beak

Using YELLOW and 3mm needles cast on 8 st

Row 1: knit
Row 2: k2tog, k4, k2tog (6)
Row 3: knit
Row 4: k2tog, k2, k2tog (4)
Row 5: knit
Row 6: k2tog twice (2)
Row 7: k2tog

Fasten off the yarn leaving an end to sew beak together.

To make up

Head

Fit the safety eyes roughly half way along the head, and approximately a quarter of the width in from the edge. Thread the yarn from the last row of the head through the stitches remaining on the needle and pull tight, then remove the stitches from the needle. With right-sides together, sew along the underside of the head, leaving a small gap at the nose for stuffing. Turn the head the right way out, and stuff to the required firmness. Sew together the remaining opening and feed the end of the yarn back through the head before cutting off. Feed the remaining end back through the head before cutting off.

Body

Thread the yarn from the last row of the body through the stitches remaining on the needle and pull tight, then remove the stitches from the needle. With right-sides together, sew along the back of the body, leaving a small gap at the bottom for stuffing. Turn the body the right way out, and stuff to the required firmness. Sew together the remaining opening and feed the end of the yarn back through the body before cutting off. Feed the remaining end back through the body before cutting off.

Legs

Thread the yarn from the last row of each claw back through the claw and cut. Fasten off the threads at the base of each claw, and then feed the ends up the leg before trimming.

Beak

Fold the beak in half, and sew together along the edge to form a triangle, leaving the cast-on edge open. Feed the thread back through the beak before trimming.

Assembly:

Attach the head to the body, making sure the nose points forward (the body seam should be at the back).

Sew the beak to the front of the head, adding a little stuffing if desired.

Using the free thread, sew the wings to the sides of the body in the position shown.

Using the free thread, attach the legs to the underside of the body.

Using the free thread, attach the tail to the back of the body, towards the bottom as shown.

Accessories

The following accessories would be suitable for Brian:

Scarf (see page 97)

AUGUST
George the Mouse

George the Mouse

Materials.

To make George you will need the following:

DK wool in grey

DK wool in pink

2 x 6mm black safety eyes

stuffing

3mm knitting needles

3mm double ended needles

embroidery needle

Head

Starting at the nose, cast on 3 st in GREY

Row 1: (inc-kw) 3 times (6)
Row 2: purl
Row 3: (inc-kw) 6 times (12)
Row 4: purl
Row 5: (inc-kw, k2, inc-kw) 3 times (18)
Row 6: purl
Row 7: k5, inc-kw, k6, inc-kw, k5 (20)
Row 8: purl
Row 9: k6, inc-kw, k6, inc-kw, k6 (22)
Row 10-20: starting and finishing with a purl row, continue in stst
Row 21: (k2tog) 11 times (11)
Row 22: (p2tog) twice, p3, (p2tog) twice (7)

Break off yarn leaving a long end and transfer stitches to a stitch holder.

Body

Starting at the base of the body, cast on 6 st in GREY

Row 1: (inc-kw) 6 times (12)
Row 2: purl
Row 3: (k1, inc-kw) 6 times (18)
Row 4: purl
Row 5: (k2, inc-kw) 6 times (24)
Row 6-26: starting and ending with a purl row, continue in stst
Row 27: (k2, k2tog) 6 times (18)
Row 28: purl
Row 29: (k1, k2tog) 6 times (12)
Row 30: purl
Row 31: (k2tog) 6 times (6)

Break off yarn leaving a long end and transfer stitches to a stitch holder.

Arms (make 2)

Using 3mm double-ended needles and leaving a long end, cast on 3 st using GREY and work i-cord as follows

Row 1: k3
Row 2: without turning the work, move the stitches to the other end of the needle, pass the wool round the back of the work. Keeping yarn tight, k3

Repeat row 2 until the arm measures 85mm.

Break off yarn leaving a long end, and transfer stitches to a stitch holder.

Legs (make 2)

Using 3mm double-ended needles and leaving a long end, cast on 4 st using GREY and work i-cord as follows

Row 1: k4
Row 2: without turning the work, move the stitches to the other end of the needle, pass the wool round the back of the work. Keeping yarn tight, k4

Repeat row 2 until the leg measures 95mm.

Break off yarn leaving a long end, and transfer stitches to a stitch holder

Tail

Using 3mm double-ended needles and leaving a long end, cast on 2 st using PINK and work i-cord as follows

Row 1: k2
Row 2: without turning the work, move the stitches to the other end of the needle, pass the wool round the back of the work. Keeping yarn tight, k2

Repeat row 2 until the tail measures 85mm.

Break off yarn leaving a long end, and transfer stitches to a stitch holder.

Ears (make 2)

Using 3mm needles cast on 2st in GREY

Row 1: (inc-kw) twice (4)
Row 2-5: knit
Row 6: (k2tog) twice (2)

Break off yarn leaving an end and transfer stitches to a stitch holder.

To make up

Head

Fit the safety eyes roughly a third of the way along the head from the nose, and roughly a quarter of the way in from each side. Thread the yarn from the last row of the head through the stitches remaining on the needle and pull tight, then remove the stitches from the needle. With right-sides together, sew along the base of the head, leaving a small gap at the nose for stuffing.
Turn the head the right way out, and stuff to the required firmness. Sew together the remaining opening and feed the end of the yarn back through the head before cutting off. Feed the remaining end back through the head before cutting off.

Body

Thread the yarn from the last row of the body through the stitches remaining on the needle and pull tight, then remove the stitches from the needle. With right-sides together, sew along the back of the body, leaving a small gap at the bottom for stuffing. Turn the body the right way out, and stuff to the required firmness.

Sew together the remaining opening and feed the end of the yarn back through the body before cutting off. Feed the remaining end back through the body before cutting off.

Arms

Thread the yarn from the last row of the arm through the stitches remaining on the needle and pull tight, then remove the stitches from the needle. Fasten off this end securely. Weave the other loose end up through the arm and cut off the excess.

Legs

Thread the yarn from the last row of the leg through the stitches remaining on the needle and pull tight, then remove the stitches from the needle. Fasten off this end securely. Weave the other loose end up through the leg and cut off the excess.

Ears

Thread the yarn from the last row of the ear through the stitches remaining on the needle and pull tight, then remove the stitches from the needle. Fasten off this end securely. Thread the other end through the ear before cutting off.

Tail

Thread the yarn from the last row of the tail through the stitches remaining on the needle and pull tight, then remove the stitches from the needle. Fasten off this end securely. Weave the other loose end up through the tail and cut off the excess.

Assembly:

Attach the head to the body, making sure the nose points forward (the body seam should be at the back)

Using the free thread, attach the arms to the body just below the head, one on each side.

Using the free thread, attach the legs to the underside of the body.

Using the free end, attach the ears to the rear of the head, one on either side as in the pictures.

Using the free thread, attach the tail to the rear of the body near the bottom.

Using a small amount of pink thread, make a few stitches at the front of the head to make a nose.

Accessories

The following accessories would be suitable for George:

Cardigan (see page 88)
Dungarees (see page 89)
Boots (see page 95)
Scarf (see page 97)

SEPTEMBER

Aster the Hedgehog

Aster the Hedgehog

Materials.

To make Aster you will need the following:

DK wool in dark brown

DK wool in light brown

DK wool in black

2 x 6mm safety eyes

stuffing

3mm knitting needles

3mm double ended needles

embroidery needle

Head

Starting at the nose and leaving a long end, cast on 3 st using BLACK

Row 1: inc-kw 3 times (6)
Row 2: purl
Row 3: inc-kw 6 times (12)
Row 4: purl
Row 5-8: continue in stst
Row 9: change to LIGHT BROWN, (inc-kw, k2, inc-kw) 3 times (18)
Row 10: purl
Row 11: k5, inc-kw, k6, inc-kw, k5 (20)
Row 12: purl
Row 13: k6, inc-kw, k6, inc-kw, k6 (22)
Row 14: purl
Row 15: k7, inc-kw, k6, inc-kw, k7 (24)
Row 16: purl
Row 17: k8, inc-kw, k6, inc-kw, k8 (26)
Row 18: purl
Row 19: change to DARK BROWN, k9, inc-kw, k6, inc-kw, k9 (28)

Row 20: starting with a purl, (p1, k1) to end
Row 21: k1, (p1, k1) 4 times, p2tog, p1, (k1, p1) twice, k1, p2tog, p1, (k1, p1) 4 times (26)
Row 22: (p1, k1) 4 times, p2tog, (k1, p1) 3 times, p2tog, (p1, k1) 4 times (24)
Row 23: k1, (p1, k1) 3 times, p2tog, (p1, k1) 3 times, p2tog, p1, (k1, p1) 3 times (22)
Row 24: (p1, k1) 4 times, (k1, p1) 3 times, k1, (k1,p1) 3 times, k1
Row 25: (k2tog, p2tog) 5 times, k2tog (11)
Row 26: p2tog, k2tog, k1, p1, k1, k2tog, p2tog (7)

Break yarn leaving a long end for sewing up the head, and place the stitches on a stitch holder.

Belly

Starting at the bottom of the belly and leaving a long end, cast on 3 st using DARK BROWN

Row 1: inc-kw 3 times (6)
Row 2: change to LIGHT BROWN and purl
Row 3: k2, (inc-kw) twice, k2 (8)
Row 4: purl
Row 5: k2, inc-kw, k2, inc-kw, k2 (10)
Row 6: purl
Row 7: k2, inc-kw, k4, inc-kw, k2 (12)
Row 8: p2, inc-pw, p6, inc-pw, p2 (14)
Row 9: knit
Row 10: purl
Row 11: knit
Row 12: purl
Row 13: k2, k2tog, k6, k2tog, k2 (12)
Row 14: p2, p2tog, p4, p2tog, p2 (10)
Row 15: k2, k2tog, k2, k2tog, k2 (8)
Row 16-24: starting and ending with a purl row, continue in stst
Row 25: k1, (k2tog, k1) twice, k1 (6)
Row 26: purl
Row 27: change to DARK BROWN, (k1, k2tog) twice (4)

Row 28: purl
Row 29: k2tog twice (2)
Row 30: cast-off kw.

Break off yarn leaving a long end.

Back

Starting at the bottom of the back and leaving a long end, cast on 5 st using DARK BROWN

Row 1: (inc-kw) 5 times (10)
Row 2: (p1, k1) 5 times
Row 3: (k1, inc-pw) 5 times (15)
Row 4: (k1, p1) 7 times, k1
Row 5: (k1, p1, inc-kw, p1, k1, inc-pw) twice, k1, p1, inc-kw (20)
Row 6: (k1, p1) 10 times
Row 7: (p1, k1) 10 times
Row 8: (k1, p1) 10 times
Row 9: (p1, k1) 10 times
Row 10: (k1, p1) 10 times
Row 11: (p1, k1) 10 times
Row 12: (k1, p1) 10 times
Row 13: (p1, k1) 10 times
Row 14: (k1, p1) 10 times
Row 15: (p1, k1) 10 times
Row 16: (k1, p1) 10 times
Row 17: (p1, k1) 10 times
Row 18: (k1, p1) 10 times
Row 19: (p1, k1) 10 times
Row 20: (k1, p1) 10 times
Row 21: (p1, k1) 10 times
Row 22: (k1, p1) 10 times
Row 23: (p1, k1) 10 times
Row 24: (k1, p1) 10 times

Row 25: (p1, k1, p2tog, k1, p1, k2tog) 2 times, p2tog, k1, p1 (15)
Row 26: (p1, k1) 7 times, p1
Row 27: (p1, k2tog) 5 times (10)
Row 28: (k1, p2tog) 3 times, k1 (7)
Row 29: (k1, p2tog) twice, k1 (5)
Row 30: cast-off kw.

Break off yarn leaving a long end.

Arms (make 2)

Starting at the top of the arm cast on 4 st using LIGHT BROWN

Row 1: inc-kw 4 times (8)
Row 2: purl
Row 3-12: continue in stst
Row 13: k2tog, inc-kw, k2, inc-kw, k2tog (8)
Row 14: purl
Row 15: k2tog, inc-kw, k2, inc-kw, k2og (8)
Row 16: purl

Break off yarn leaving a long end to sew up the arm, and transfer stitches to a stitch holder.

Legs (make 2)

Using 3mm double-ended needles and leaving a long end, cast on 4 st using LIGHT BROWN and work i-cord as follows

Row 1: k4
Row 2: without turning the work, move the stitches to the other end of the needle, pass the wool round the back of the work. Keeping yarn tight, k4

Repeat row 2 until the leg measures 80mm.
Transfer to a stitch holder.

Ears (make 2)

Cast on 4 st using LIGHT BROWN

Row 1-3: knit
Row 4: (k2tog) twice (2)
Row 5: cast-off

Shoes (make 2)

Cast on 14 st using DARK BROWN

Row 1-2: knit
Row 3: K3, (k2tog) 4 times, K3 (10)

Row 4: K3, (k2tog) twice, K3 (8)
Row 5-6: knit
Row 7: cast-off kw.
Break off yarn leaving a long end.

To make up

Head

Fit the safety eyes close together just behind the nose as shown in the pictures. Thread the yarn from the last row of the head through the stitches remaining on the needle and pull tight, then remove the stitches from the needle. With right-sides together, sew along the underside of the head, leaving a small gap at the nose for stuffing. Turn the head the right way out, and stuff to the required firmness. Sew together the remaining opening and feed the end of the yarn back through the head before cutting off. Feed the remaining end back through the head before cutting off.

Body

With right sides together, sew the belly to the back down each side. Run a thread round the neck using a running stitch and gather, then fasten off.
Turn the body right-side out and stuff.
Sew up the bottom opening.
Thread the remaining end back up through the body before cutting off.

Arms

Thread the yarn from the last row of the arm through the stitches remaining on the needle and pull tight, then remove the stitches from the needle. With right-sides together, sew along the underside of the arm, leaving a small gap at the end. Turn the arm inside out and sew up the remaining opening. Fasten off this end

securely and feed back through the arm before cutting off. Weave the other loose end up through the arm and cut off the excess.

Legs

Thread the yarn from the last row of the leg through the stitches remaining on the needle and pull tight, then remove the stitches from the needle. Fasten off this end securely. Weave the other loose end up through the leg and cut off the excess.

Shoes

Fold the shoe in half and sew along the bottom of the shoe and up the back. Fasten off the ends and feed back through the shoe before cutting off.

Assembly:

Attach the head to the body, making sure the nose points in the same direction as the stomach of the hedgehog.

Using the free thread, attach the arms to the body just below the head, one on each side.

Feed the each leg into a shoe and fasten with a small stitch. Then using the free thread, attach the legs to the underside of the body, making sure the toes are facing forward.

Using the free thread, attach the ears to the head.

Accessories

I would suggest the following accessories for Aster:

Shawl (see page 97)
Scarf (see page 97)

OCTOBER

Bertie the Badger

Bertie the Badger

Materials.

To make Bertie you will need the following:

DK wool in black

DK wool in white

2 x 6mm safety eyes

stuffing

3mm knitting needles

3mm double ended needles

embroidery needle

Back

Starting at the bottom of the back and leaving a long end, cast on 5 st using GREY

Row 1: inc-kw 5 times (10)
Row 2: purl
Row 3: (k1, inc-kw) 5 times (15)
Row 4: purl
Row 5: (k2, inc-kw, k2, inc-kw) twice, k2, inc-kw (20)
Row 6: purl
Row 7-24: starting with a knit row, continue in stst
Row 25: (k2, k2tog) 4 times, k2tog, k2 (15)
Row 26: purl
Row 27: (k1, k2tog) 5 times (10)
Row 28: (p1, p2tog) 3 times, p1 (7)
Row 29: (k1, k2tog) twice, k1 (5)
Row 30: cast-off pw.

Break off yarn leaving a long end.

Head.

Using 3mm needles and BLACK cast on 10 st

Row 1: k2, inc-kw, k4, inc-kw, k2 (12)
Row 2: purl
Row 3: knit
Row 4: change to WHITE and purl
Row 5: k2, inc-kw, k6, inc-kw, k2 (14)
Row 6: change to BLACK and purl
Row 7: knit
Row 8: p2, inc-pw, p8, inc-pw, p2 (16)
Row 9: knit
Row 10: change to WHITE and purl
Row 11: knit
Row 12: purl
Row 13: change to BLACK and knit
Row 14: p2, p2tog, p8, p2tog, p2 (14)
Row 15: knit
Row 16: purl
Row 17: change to WHITE and k2, k2tog, k6, k2tog, k2 (12)
Row 18: purl
Row 19: change to BLACK and knit
Row 20: purl
Row 21: k2, k2tog, k4, k2tog, k2 (10)
Row 22: cast off kw

Belly

Starting at the bottom of the belly and leaving a long end, cast on 3 st using BLACK

Row 1: inc-kw 3 times (6)
Row 2: purl
Row 3: k2, (inc-kw) twice, k2 (8)
Row 4: purl

Row 5: k2, inc-kw, k2, inc-kw, k2 (10)
Row 6: purl
Row 7: k2, inc-kw, k4, inc-kw, k2 (12)
Row 8: p2, inc-pw, p6, inc-pw, p2 (14)
Row 9: knit
Row 10: purl
Row 11: knit
Row 12: purl
Row 13: k2, k2tog, k6, k2tog, k2 (12)
Row 14: p2, p2tog, p4, p2tog, p2 (10)
Row 15: k2, k2tog, k2, k2tog, k2 (8)
Row 16-24: starting and ending with a purl row, continue in stst
Row 25: k1, (k2tog, k1) twice, k1 (6)
Row 26: purl
Row 27: (k1, k2tog) twice (4)
Row 28: purl
Row 29: k2tog twice (2)
Row 30: cast-off kw.

Break off yarn leaving a long end.

Ears (make 2)

Cast on 6 st using BLACK

Row 1-3: knit
Row 4: k2tog, k2, k2tog (4)
Row 5: (k2tog) twice (2)
Row 6: k2tog (1)
Row 7:Cast off.

Break off yarn leaving a long end.

Arms (make 2)

Using 3mm double-ended needles and leaving a long end, cast on 3 st using BLACK and work i-cord as follows

Row 1: k3
Row 2: without turning the work, move the stitches to the other end of the needle, pass the wool round the back of the work. Keeping yarn tight, k3

Repeat row 2 until the arm measures 55mm.

Break off yarn leaving a long end, and transfer stitches to a stitch holder.

Legs (make 2)

Using 3mm double-ended needles and leaving a long end, cast on 4 st using BLACK and work i-cord as follows

Row 1: k4
Row 2: without turning the work, move the stitches to the other end of the needle, pass the wool round the back of the work. Keeping yarn tight, k4

Repeat row 2 until the leg measures 95mm.

Break off yarn leaving a long end, and transfer stitches to a stitch holder.

To make up

Head

Fit the safety eyes roughly a third of the way along the head, in the centre of the black stripes. Fold the head in half so that the stripes run from the front to the back of the head and with right-sides together, sew along the underside of the head, leaving a small gap at the nose for stuffing. Turn the head the right way out, and stuff to the required firmness. Sew together the remaining opening and feed the end of the yarn back through the head before cutting off. Feed the remaining end back through the head before cutting off.

Body

With right sides together, sew the belly to the back down each side. Run a thread round the neck using a running stitch and gather, then fasten off.
Turn the body right-side out and stuff.
Sew up the bottom opening.
Thread the remaining end back up through the body before cutting off.

Legs

Thread the yarn from the last row of the leg through the stitches remaining on the needle and pull tight, then remove the stitches from the needle. Fasten off this end securely. Weave the other loose end up through the leg and cut off the excess.

Arms

Thread the yarn from the last row of the arm through the stitches remaining on the needle and pull tight, then remove the stitches from the needle. Fasten off this end securely. Weave the other loose end up through the leg and cut off the excess.

Assembly:

Attach the head to the body, making sure the nose points in the same direction as the stomach of the badger.

Using the free thread, attach the arms to the body just below the head, one on each side.

Using the free thread, attach the legs to the underside of the body.

Using the free thread, attach the ears to the head.

Using a small amount of black thread, make a few stitches at the front of the head to make a nose.

Accessories

I would suggest the following accessories for Bertie:

Dungarees (see page 89)
Waistcoat (see page 96)

NOVEMBER

Sidney the Squirrel

Sidney the Squirrel

Materials.

To make Sidney you will need the following:

DK wool in red

DK wool in white

DK wool in black

2 x 6mm safety eyes

stuffing

3mm knitting needles

3mm double ended needles

embroidery needle

For loop stitch see page 98

Belly

Starting at the bottom of the belly and leaving a long end, cast on 2 st using RED

Row 1: (inc-kw) twice (4)
Row 2: change to WHITE and purl
Row 3: k1, (inc-kw) twice, k1 (6)
Row 4: purl
Row 5: k2, (inc-kw) twice, k2 (8)
Row 6: purl
Row 7: k2, inc-kw, k2, inc-kw, k2 (10)
Row 8: p2, inc-pw, p4, inc-pw, p2 (12)
Row 9: knit
Row 10: purl
Row 11: knit
Row 12: purl
Row 13: k2, k2tog, k4, k2tog, k2 (10)
Row 14: p2, p2tog, p2, p2tog, p2 (8)
Row 15: k2, (k2tog) twice, k2 (6)
Row 16-22: starting and ending with a purl row, continue in stst
Row 23: k1, (k2tog) twice, k1 (4)

Row 24: purl
Row 25: change to RED, (k2tog) twice (2)
Row 26: purl
Row 27: knit
Row 28: cast-off kw.

Break off yarn leaving a long end.

Back

Starting at the bottom of the back and leaving a long end, cast on 5 st using RED

Row 1: inc-kw 5 times (10)
Row 2: purl
Row 3: (k1, inc-kw) 5 times (15)
Row 4: purl
Row 5: (k2, inc-kw, k2, inc-w) twice, k2, inc-kw (20)
Row 6: purl
Row 7-22: starting with a knit row, continue in stst
Row 23: (k2, k2tog) 4 times, k2tog, k2 (15)
Row 24: purl
Row 25: (k1, k2tog) 5 times (10)
Row 26: (p1, p2tog) 3 times, p1 (7)
Row 27: (k1, k2tog) twice, k1 (5)
Row 28: cast-off pw.

Break off yarn leaving a long end.

Head

Starting at the nose, cast on 3 st in RED

Row 1: (inc-kw) 3 times (6)
Row 2: purl

Row 3: (inc-kw) 6 times (12)
Row 4: purl
Row 5: (inc-kw, k2, inc-kw) 3 times (18)
Row 6: purl
Row 7: k5, inc-kw, k6, inc-kw, k5 (20)
Row 8: purl
Row 9: k6, inc-kw, k6, inc-kw, k6 (22)
Row 10-20: starting and ending with a purl row, continue in stst
Row 21: (k2tog) 11 times (11)
Row 22: (p2tog) twice, p3, (p2tog) twice (7)

Break off yarn leaving a long end and transfer stitches to a stitch holder.

Arms (make 2)

Using 3mm double-ended needles and leaving a long end, cast on 3 st using RED and work i-cord as follows

Row 1: k3
Row 2: without turning the work, move the stitches to the other end of the needle, pass the wool round the back of the work. Keeping yarn tight, k3

Repeat row 2 until the arm measures 85mm.

Break off yarn leaving a long end, and transfer stitches to a stitch holder

Tail

Starting at the base of the tail cast on 4 st in RED

Row 1: inc-kw 4 times (8)
Row 2: purl
Row 3: k1, loop st 6 times, k1
Row 4: purl
Row 5: k1, loop st 6 times, k1
Row 6: purl
Row 7: k1, loop st 6 times, k1
Row 8: purl
Row 9: k1, loop st 6 times, k1
Row 10: purl
Row 11: k1, loop st 6 times, k1
Row 12: purl
Row 13: k1, loop st 6 times, k1
Row 14: purl
Row 15: k1, loop st 6 times, k1
Row 16: purl
Row 17: k1, loop st 6 times, k1
Row 18: purl
Row 19: k1, loop st 6 times, k1
Row 20: purl
Row 21: k1, loop st 6 times, k1
Row 22: purl
Row 23: k2tog 4 times (4)

Break yarn leaving long end and transfer stitches to a stitch holder.

Ears (make 2)

Cast on 6 st using RED

Row 1-3: knit
Row 4: k2tog, k2, k2tog (4)
Row 5: (k2tog) twice (2)
Row 6: k2tog (1)
Row 7: Cast off.

Legs (make 2)

Using 3mm double-ended needles and leaving a long end, cast on 4 st using RED and work i-cord as follows

Row 1: k4
Row 2: without turning the work, move the stitches to the other end of the needle, pass the wool round the back of the work. Keeping yarn tight, k4

Repeat row 2 until the leg measures 95mm.

Break off yarn leaving a long end, and transfer stitches to a stitch holder.

To make up

Head

Fit the safety eyes roughly half way along the head, and approximately a quarter of the width in from the edge. Thread the yarn from the last row of the head through the stitches remaining on the needle and pull tight, then remove the stitches from the needle. With right-sides together, sew along the underside of the head, leaving a small gap at the nose for stuffing. Turn the head the right way out, and stuff to the required firmness. Sew together the remaining opening and feed the end of the yarn back through the head before cutting off. Feed the remaining end back through the head before cutting off.

Body

With right sides together, sew the belly to the back down each side. Run a thread round the neck using a running stitch and gather, then fasten off.
Turn the body right-side out and stuff.
Sew up the bottom opening.
Thread the remaining end back up through the body before cutting off.

Arms

Thread the yarn from the last row of the arm through the stitches remaining on the needle and pull tight, then remove the stitches from the needle. Fasten off this end securely. Weave the other loose end up through the arm and cut off the excess.

Legs

Thread the yarn from the last row of the leg through the stitches remaining on the needle and pull tight, then remove the stitches from the needle. Fasten off this end securely. Weave the other loose end up through the leg and cut off the excess.

Ears

Fasten off the end at the top of the ear, and weave through the ear before cutting off.

Tail

Fold the tail in half with the loops on the outside. Sew up the edge of the tail. Fasten off and pass the free end of the yarn up through the tail before trimming off.

Assembly:

Attach the head to the body, making sure the nose points in the same direction as the stomach of the squirrel.

Using the free thread, attach the arms to the body just below the head, one on each side.

Using the free thread, attach the legs to the underside of the body.

Using the free thread, attach the tail to the rear of the body near the bottom.

Using the free thread, attach the ears to the sides of the head as shown.

Using a small amount of black thread, make a few stitches at the front of the head to make a nose.

Accessories

I would suggest the following accessories for Sidney:

Cardigan (see page 88)
Scarf (see page 97)

DECEMBER

Noel the Robin

Noel the Robin

Materials

To make Noel you will need the following:

DK wool in white red and brown

2 x 6mm black safety eyes

stuffing

3mm knitting needles

3mm double ended needles

embroidery needle

Head

Starting at the front of the head and leaving a long end, cast on 3 st using RED and 3mm needles

Row 1: inc-kw 3 times (6)
Row 2: purl
Row 3: inc-kw 6 times (12)
Row 4: purl
Row 5: (inc-kw, k2, inc-kw) 3 times (18)
Row 6: purl
Row 7: k5, inc-kw, k6 inc-kw, k5 (20)
Row 8: Purl
Row 9: K6, inc-kw, k6, inc-kw, k6 (22)
Row 10: purl
Row 11: knit
Row 12: purl
Row 13: change to brown, knit
Row 14: purl
Row 15: knit
Row 16: purl
Row 17: k2tog 11 times (11)
Row 18: p2tog twice, p3, p2tog twice (7)

Break yarn leaving a long end for sewing up the head, and place the stitches on a stitch holder.

Body

Starting at the base of the body cast on 6 st using WHITE and 3mm needles

Row 1: inc-kw 6 times (12)
Row 2: purl
Row 3: (k1, inc-kw) 6 times (18)
Row 4: purl
Row 5: (K2, inc-kw) 6 times (24)
Row 6: purl
Row 7: knit
Row 8: purl
Row 9: change to RED, knit
Row 10-20: starting and ending with a purl row, continue in stst
Row 21: (k2, k2tog) 6 times (18)
Row 22: purl
Row 23: (k1, k2tog) 6 times (12)
Row 24: purl
Row 25: k2tog 6 times (6)

Break off yarn leaving a long end to sew up body, and transfer stitches to a stitch holder.

Legs (make 2)

Using 3mm double-ended needles and leaving a long end, cast on 4 st in BROWN and work i-cord as follows

Row 1: k4
Row 2: without turning the work, move the stitches to the other end of the needle, pass the wool round the back of the work. Keeping yarn tight, k4

Repeat row 2 until the leg measures 95mm.

Claws: continue in brown

Row 1: inc-kw
Put the remaining stitches on a stitch holder, then continue working on these 2 stitches as for the leg, working 4 rows in total.
Cast off kw. Break yarn leaving an end.

Re-join yarn and work the same on the next 2 stiches for a total of 4 rows.
Cast off kw. Break yarn leaving an end.
Rejoin yarn into last st and inc-kw.
Wor 4 rows in total on these 2 stitches.
Cast-off kw leaving an end.

Wings (Make 2)

Using BROWN and 3mm needles cast on 3 st.

Row 1: inc-kw, k2 (4)
Row 2: knit
Row 3: inc-kw, k3 (5)
Row 4: knit
Row 5: knit
Row 6: knit
Row 7: inc-kw, k4 (6)
Row 8: knit
Row 9: knit
Row 10: knit
Row 11: inc-kw, k5 (7)
Row 12: k6, inc-kw (8)
Row 13: inc-kw, k7 (9)
Row 14: k8, inc-kw (10)
Row 15: inc-kw, k9 (11)
Row 16: knit
Row 17: k2tog, k7, k2tog (9)
Row 18: k2tog, k5, k2tog (7)
Row 19: k2tog, k3, k2tog (5)
Row 20: k2tog, k1, k2tog (3)
cast off kw. Break yarn leaving an end for sewing the wing to the body.

Tail

Using BROWN and 3mm needles cast on 2 st

Row 1: inc-kw twice (4)
Rows 2-6: knit
Break off yarn and leave stiches on needle

Cast on 2 st
Row 1: inc-kw twice (4)
Rows 2-6: knit
Row 7: knit across both tail sections (8)

Rows 8-12: knit
Row 13: k2tog, 4, k2tog (6)

cast off kw. Break yarn leaving an end to sew tail on to the body.

Beak

Using BROWN and 3mm needles cast on 8 st

Row 1: knit
Row 2: k2tog, k4, k2tog (6)
Row 3: knit
Row 4: k2tog, k2, k2tog (4)
Row 5: knit
Row 6: k2tog twice (2)
Row 7: k2tog
Fasten off the yarn leaving an end to sew beak together.

To make up

Head

Fit the safety eyes roughly half way along the head, and approximately a quarter of the width in from the edge. Thread the yarn from the last row of the head through the stitches remaining on the needle and pull tight, then remove the stitches from the needle. With right-sides together, sew along the underside of the head, leaving a small gap at the nose for stuffing. Turn the head the right way out, and stuff to the required firmness. Sew together the remaining opening and feed the end of the yarn back through the head before cutting off. Feed the remaining end back through the head before cutting off.

Body

Thread the yarn from the last row of the body through the stitches remaining on the needle and pull tight, then remove the stitches from the needle. With right-sides together, sew along the back of the body, leaving a small gap at the bottom for stuffing. Turn the body the right way out, and stuff to the required firmness. Sew together the remaining opening and feed the end of the yarn back through the body before cutting off. Feed the remaining end back through the body before cutting off.

Legs

Thread the yarn from the last row of each claw back through the claw and cut. fasten off the threads at the base of each claw, and then feed the ends up the leg before trimming.

Beak

Fold the beak in half, and sew together along the edge to form a triangle, leaving the cast-on edge open. Feed the thread back through the beak before trimming.

Assembly:

Attach the head to the body, making sure the nose points forward (the body seam should be at the back).

Sew the beak to the front of the head, adding a little stuffing if desired.

Using the free thread, sew the wings to the sides of the body in the position shown.

Using the free thread, attach the legs to the underside of the body.

Using the free thread, attach the tail to the back of the body, towards the bottom as shown.

Accessories

The following accessories would be suitable for Noel:

Scarf (see page 97)

Clothes

Cardigan

Materials

Double knitting in your chosen colour

3mm needles

stitch holder / spare needle

Sleeves (knit 2)

Using 3mm needles cast on 9 st

Row 1-9: st-st
Row 10: cast off 1 pw, p7 (8st)
Row 11: cast off 1, k6 (7 st)

Break off yarn and place remaining stitches on a spare needle or stitch holder.

Body

Using 3mm needles, cast on 24 st

Row 1: (k1, p1) 12 times
Row 2: (p1, k1) 12 times
Row 3-11: continue in stst, starting and ending with k row
Row 12: p5, cast off 2 pw, p10, cast off 2 pw, p 5 (20)
Row 13: k5, k7 across first sleeve, k10, k7 across second sleeve, k5 (34)
Row 14: purl
Row 15: k2, k2tog, k1, k2tog, k3, k2tog, k1, k2tog, k4, k2tog, k1, k2tog, k3, k2tog, k1, k2tog, k2 (26)
Row 16: purl
Row 17: k1, k2tog, k1, k2tog, k1, k2tog, k1, k2tog, k2, k2tog, k1, k2tog, k1, k2tog, k1, k2tog, k1 (18)
Row 18: purl
Row 19: cast off kw.

Break off yarn and fasten off.

Assembly

Turn sleeves inside out and sew underarm seam, making sure you stop before the shaping starts.

Sew sleeve to body.

Darn in all loose ends, then fasten buttons as required down front of cardigan.

Dungarees

Materials

Double knitting in your chosen colour

3mm needles

stitch holder / spare needle

Legs (make 2)

Using 3mm needles cast on 17st

Row 1-10: beginning with a knit row, work in stst
For first leg, break off yarn and leave stiches on
needle. For second leg, do not break yarn and
continue as follows:

Waist section

Row 1: k17 across second leg, then continue to k17
across first leg (34)
Row 2: purl
Row 3-16: continuing with a knit row work 14 rows stst

Bib

Row 1: cast off 13 st kw, k20 (21)
Row 2: cast-off 13 st purl-wise, k7 (8)
Row 3-7: beginning with a knit row, work 5 rows stst
Row 8: cast-off kw.

Straps (make 2)

Using 3mm double-ended needles and leaving a long
end, cast on 2 st and work i-cord as follows

Row 1: k2
Row 2: without turning the work, move the stitches to
the other end of the needle, pass the wool round the
back of the work. Keeping yarn tight, k2

Repeat row 2 until the strap measures 95mm

Cast off kw.

Assembly

To assemble the dungarees, fold with right-sides
together so that the sides of the waist section meet in
the centre back of the dungarees.

Sew up each leg seam until you reach the crotch, then join the back seam. Fasten off the loose ends before weaving them in and trimming.

If making the dungarees for a mouse, leave a small gap in the back seam for the tail to stick through.

Turn the dungarees the right way out, and attach a strap to each corner of the bib. Cross over the straps and fasten approximately 4st from the back seam as shown below.

Fasten off and weave in all loose ends before trimming.

Jumper

Materials

Double knitting in your chosen colour

3mm needles

stich holder / spare needle

Body (make 2)

Cast on 18 st

Row 1-3: (k1, p1) to end
Row 4-10: starting and ending with a purl row, continue in stst
Row 11: k2tog, k14, k2tog (16)
Row 12: purl
Row 13: k2tog, k12, k2tog (14)
Row 14: p2tog, p10, p2tog (12)
Row 15: knit
Row 16: p2tog, p8, p2tog (10)
Row 17: k2tog, k6, k2tog (8)
Row 18: purl
Cast-off knit-wise

Arms (make 2)

Cast on 12 st

Row 1-3: (k1, p1 to end)
Row 4-10: starting and ending with a purl row, continue in stst
Row 11: k2tog, k8, k2tog (10)
Row 12: purl
Row 13: k2tog, k6, k2tog (8)

Row 14: purl
Row 15: k2tog, k4, k2tog (6)
Row 16: purl
Row 17: k2tog, k2, k2tog (4)
Row 18: purl

Cast-off knit-wise

Assembly

Sleeves:

With right-sides together, sew the straight portion of the sleeve together, making sure you stop when the shaping starts. Fasten off the end.

Body:

With right-sides of the two body pieces together, sew the side seams of the body, making sure you stop when the shaping begins.

Joining together:

Turn the sleeves the right way out. Put a sleeve on the inside of the body, and join the sleeve to the body by sewing round the sleeve. Note the top of the sleeve forms the shoulder of the jumper.

Repeat for the other sleeve.

Fasten off and weave in all ends before trimming.

Turn the jumper the right way out.

Dress

Materials

A small amount of your chosen material

Small press-stud fastener

Needle and thread

1. Draw or copy the pattern pieces from page 94 onto paper or card and cut out. Make sure you mark the crosses on the pattern pieces

2. Place the pattern pieces onto the material and draw round them, then cut out the pieces leaving 5mm seam allowance around the pattern. When cutting out the back pieces, fold the material right sides together first so that you end up with a right and left piece.

3. To stop the edges fraying, run a zig-zag stitch round the edge of each piece using a sewing machine.

4. Placing right-sides together, join the sides to the front of the dress up to the cross mark.

5. Press the seams open, then sew round the arm holes.

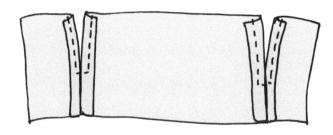

6. Fold over and sew the bottom hem on the skirt. Then thread a running stitch along the top edge and gather to the same width as the top of the dress.

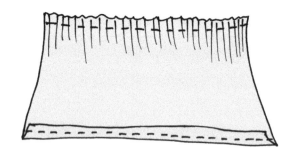

7. Putting right-sides together, join the skirt to the bottom edge of the dress body.

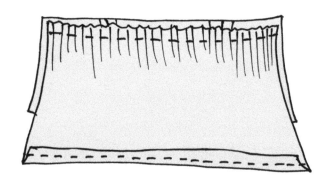

8. Press the dress with the waist seam facing downwards, then fold over and stitch the seams down the sides of the dress.

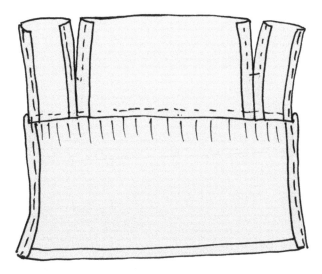

10. With right-sides outside, oversew the shoulders as shown, and then attach a small press-stud to join the two halfs of the back together.

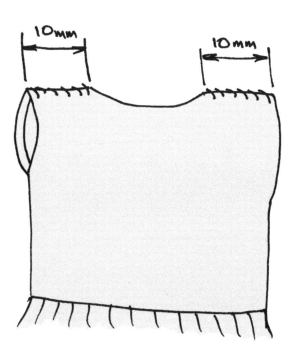

9. Turn over and sew the edges of the shoulders and neck.

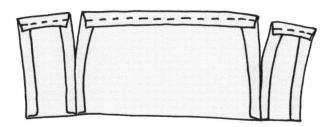

Dress Pattern Pieces

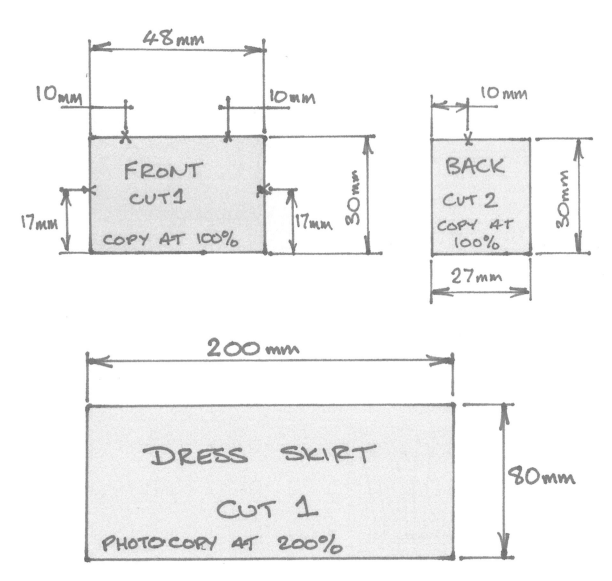

48mm

10mm   10mm

FRONT
CUT1

17mm   17mm   30mm

COPY AT 100%

10mm

BACK

CUT 2

COPY AT
100%

30mm

27mm

200 mm

DRESS SKIRT

CUT 1

PHOTOCOPY AT 200%

80mm

Add 5mm seam allowance to ALL sides

Boots

Materials

Double knitting wool in your chosen colour
4mm needles

Boots (make 2)

Using 4mm needles cast on 14 st in your chosen colour

Row 1-2: knit
Row 3: K3, K2tog 4 times, K3 (10)
Row 4: K3, K2tog twice, K3 (8)
Row 5-6: knit
cast-off knit-wise.

Break off yarn leaving a long end.

To make up

Fold the boot in half and stitch down the back and along the bottom of the boot.

Hare Shoes

Materials

Double knitting in your chosen colour
3mm needles

Shoes (make 2)

Using 3mm needles cast on 28 st in your chosen colour

Row 1-6: work in stst beginning with a knit row
Row 7: k6, (k2tog) 8 times, k6 (20)
Row 8: p6, (p2tog) 4 times, p6 (16)
Row 9: k5, (k2tog) 3 times, k5 (13)
Row 10: p5, p2tog, p6 (12)
cast off knit-wise

Break off yarn leaving a long end.

To make up

With right-sides together, sew along the sole and up the back of the shoe.
Fasten off ends and feed through the seams.
Turn right-side out.

Waistcoat

Materials

Double knitting in your chosen colour
3mm needles
Stitch holder

Using 3mm needles, cast on 28st

Row 1: (k1, p1) 14 times
Row 2: (p1, k1) 14 times
Row 3-11: starting and ending with a knit row, continue in stst
Row 12: p8, cast-off 2 pw, p10, cast-off 2 pw, p6 (24)

Right front:

Row 1: k7 (7)
Row 2: p7
Row 3: k2tog, k5 (6)
Row 4: p6
Row 5: k2tog, k3, inc-kw (6)
put these stitches on a stitch holder

Back:

Row 1-4: Rejoin yarn and beginning with a knit row, continue in stst on the next 10 st (10)
Row 5: inc-kw, k8, inc-kw (12)
Put these stitches on a stitch holder

Left front:

Row 1: re-join yarn and k7 (7)
Row 2: p7
Row 3: k5, k2tog (6)
Row 4: p6
Row 5: inc-kw, k3, k2tog (6)

Join together

Row 1: k6, k12 across the back, k6 across the right front (24)
Row 2: cast-off kw.

Sew in the ends before trimming them.

Scarf

Shawl

Materials

Double knitting in your chosen colour

3mm needles

Scarf

using 3mm needles cast on 5st

Row 1: k1, p1, k1, p1, k1

Repeat row 1 until the scarf reaches the required length (I find approximately 210mm looks good).

Cast-off kw.

Sew in ends before trimming.

Materials

Double knitting in your chosen colour

7mm needles

Using 7mm needles, cast on 20st

Row 1: knit
Row 2: k2tog, knit to end

Repeat row 2 until you have 1 st left. Fasten off then sew in ends before trimming.

Loop Stitch

1. Start to knit the stitch as normal, but stop before you slip the stitch off the needle.

2. Bring the wool forward between the needles, round your left thumb, then back between the needles.

3. Pass the first loop of the stitch from the right needle to the left.

4. Knit BOTH loops of the stitch together by pushing the right needle through the loops from left to right.

5. Wrap the wool round the right needle then finish knitting the stitch.

6. As you slip the stitch off the needle pull the loop tight to secure it.

If you are having trouble following these instructions, there are plenty of videos available on the internet to show you several methods to produce a loop stitch.

A Huge 'Thank you'!

I have an amazing family and a very supportive husband! Without my husband this book would not have been published.

This book is for Benjamin and Carly. I am very proud of you both and I hope you are proud of your mum who has done something off her bucket list.

I would like to thank the lovely group of ladies who helped with proof knitting my patterns for me: Lesley Brown, Margaret Humphreys, Pat Thomas and Mary Martin. Without your help I would still be sat here knitting frogs legs or robins beaks.

Finally, I would like to thank Beercott Books for believing I could do this.

Kerry

Lightning Source UK Ltd.
Milton Keynes UK
UKHW05f0241030518
321994UK00008B/165/P